50 Sundae Split Recipes for Home

By: Kelly Johnson

Table of Contents

- Classic Banana Split
- Strawberry Shortcake Split
- Chocolate Fudge Sundae Split
- Peanut Butter Cup Split
- Rocky Road Sundae Split
- Salted Caramel Banana Split
- Tropical Fruit Split
- S'mores Sundae Split
- Mint Chocolate Chip Split
- Cookie Dough Sundae Split
- Brownie Sundae Split
- Nutella Hazelnut Split
- Berry Blast Split
- Mocha Almond Fudge Split
- Key Lime Pie Split
- Caramel Apple Split
- Lemon Meringue Sundae Split
- Cookies and Cream Split
- Chocolate Mint Split
- Maple Pecan Split
- Cherry Cheesecake Split
- Coffee Crunch Split
- Pumpkin Spice Split
- Tiramisu Sundae Split
- Matcha Green Tea Split
- Raspberry Sorbet Split
- Almond Joy Split
- Peanut Butter Banana Split
- Pina Colada Split
- Chocolate Chip Cookie Split
- Cinnamon Roll Sundae Split
- Chocolate Strawberry Split
- Maple Bacon Split
- Key Lime Coconut Split
- Raspberry White Chocolate Split
- Dark Chocolate Cherry Split
- Pistachio Dream Split
- Orange Creamsicle Split
- Snickers Sundae Split

- Lemon Basil Split
- Red Velvet Cake Split
- Fudge Brownie Split
- Coconut Cream Pie Split
- Orange Mango Split
- Vanilla Almond Joy Split
- Tropical Paradise Split
- Butterscotch Pecan Split
- Strawberry Cheesecake Split
- Chocolate Coconut Split
- Vanilla Bourbon Split

Classic Banana Split

Ingredients:

- 1 banana, halved lengthwise
- 2 scoops vanilla ice cream
- 2 scoops chocolate ice cream
- 2 scoops strawberry ice cream
- Chocolate syrup
- Whipped cream
- Maraschino cherries
- Chopped nuts (optional)

Instructions:

1. Place the banana halves in a dish, cut side up.
2. Add scoops of vanilla, chocolate, and strawberry ice cream between the banana halves.
3. Drizzle with chocolate syrup and top with whipped cream, a cherry, and nuts.

Strawberry Shortcake Split

Ingredients:

- 1 banana, halved lengthwise
- 2 scoops vanilla ice cream
- 1 cup fresh strawberries, sliced
- Strawberry sauce
- Whipped cream

Instructions:

1. Place banana halves in a dish, cut side up.
2. Add scoops of vanilla ice cream on top.
3. Top with sliced strawberries and drizzle with strawberry sauce.
4. Finish with a dollop of whipped cream.

Chocolate Fudge Sundae Split

Ingredients:

- 1 banana, halved lengthwise
- 2 scoops chocolate ice cream
- Hot fudge sauce
- Whipped cream
- Chocolate sprinkles
- Maraschino cherries

Instructions:

1. Place banana halves in a dish.
2. Add scoops of chocolate ice cream.
3. Drizzle hot fudge sauce on top.
4. Garnish with whipped cream, chocolate sprinkles, and a cherry.

Peanut Butter Cup Split

Ingredients:

- 1 banana, halved lengthwise
- 2 scoops chocolate ice cream
- 2 tablespoons peanut butter
- Hot fudge sauce
- Whipped cream
- Crushed peanut butter cups

Instructions:

1. Place banana halves in a dish, cut side up.
2. Add scoops of chocolate ice cream.
3. Drizzle with peanut butter and hot fudge sauce.
4. Top with whipped cream and crushed peanut butter cups.

Rocky Road Sundae Split

Ingredients:

- 1 banana, halved lengthwise
- 2 scoops rocky road ice cream
- Marshmallow fluff
- Chopped nuts
- Whipped cream
- Chocolate syrup

Instructions:

1. Place banana halves in a dish.
2. Add scoops of rocky road ice cream.
3. Drizzle with marshmallow fluff and chocolate syrup.
4. Top with whipped cream and chopped nuts.

Salted Caramel Banana Split

Ingredients:

- 1 banana, halved lengthwise
- 2 scoops vanilla ice cream
- Salted caramel sauce
- Whipped cream
- Sea salt for garnish

Instructions:

1. Place banana halves in a dish.
2. Add scoops of vanilla ice cream.
3. Drizzle with salted caramel sauce.
4. Top with whipped cream and a sprinkle of sea salt.

Tropical Fruit Split

Ingredients:

- 1 banana, halved lengthwise
- 2 scoops coconut ice cream
- Fresh pineapple chunks
- Mango slices
- Toasted coconut flakes
- Whipped cream

Instructions:

1. Place banana halves in a dish.
2. Add scoops of coconut ice cream.
3. Top with pineapple and mango.
4. Garnish with toasted coconut flakes and whipped cream.

S'mores Sundae Split

Ingredients:

- 1 banana, halved lengthwise
- 2 scoops vanilla ice cream
- Graham cracker crumbs
- Mini marshmallows
- Chocolate syrup
- Whipped cream

Instructions:

1. Place banana halves in a dish.
2. Add scoops of vanilla ice cream.
3. Sprinkle with graham cracker crumbs and mini marshmallows.
4. Drizzle with chocolate syrup and top with whipped cream.

Enjoy these delicious splits and sundaes!

Mint Chocolate Chip Split

Ingredients:

- 1 banana, halved lengthwise
- 2 scoops mint chocolate chip ice cream
- Chocolate syrup
- Whipped cream
- Chocolate shavings or chips
- Fresh mint leaves for garnish

Instructions:

1. Place banana halves in a dish, cut side up.
2. Add scoops of mint chocolate chip ice cream on top.
3. Drizzle with chocolate syrup.
4. Top with whipped cream, chocolate shavings, and garnish with fresh mint leaves.

Cookie Dough Sundae Split

Ingredients:

- 1 banana, halved lengthwise
- 2 scoops vanilla ice cream
- Cookie dough pieces (store-bought or homemade)
- Chocolate syrup
- Whipped cream
- Mini chocolate chips

Instructions:

1. Place banana halves in a dish.
2. Add scoops of vanilla ice cream.
3. Scatter cookie dough pieces over the ice cream.
4. Drizzle with chocolate syrup and top with whipped cream and mini chocolate chips.

Brownie Sundae Split

Ingredients:

- 1 banana, halved lengthwise
- 2 scoops chocolate ice cream
- 1 brownie, cut into pieces
- Hot fudge sauce
- Whipped cream
- Chopped nuts (optional)

Instructions:

1. Place banana halves in a dish.
2. Add scoops of chocolate ice cream on top.
3. Top with brownie pieces and drizzle with hot fudge sauce.
4. Finish with whipped cream and chopped nuts if desired.

Nutella Hazelnut Split

Ingredients:

- 1 banana, halved lengthwise
- 2 scoops hazelnut ice cream
- Nutella, for drizzling
- Whipped cream
- Chopped hazelnuts

Instructions:

1. Place banana halves in a dish.
2. Add scoops of hazelnut ice cream.
3. Drizzle with Nutella.
4. Top with whipped cream and sprinkle with chopped hazelnuts.

Berry Blast Split

Ingredients:

- 1 banana, halved lengthwise
- 2 scoops vanilla ice cream
- Mixed fresh berries (strawberries, blueberries, raspberries)
- Berry sauce (optional)
- Whipped cream

Instructions:

1. Place banana halves in a dish.
2. Add scoops of vanilla ice cream.
3. Top with mixed fresh berries and drizzle with berry sauce if using.
4. Finish with whipped cream.

Mocha Almond Fudge Split

Ingredients:

- 1 banana, halved lengthwise
- 2 scoops mocha almond fudge ice cream
- Hot fudge sauce
- Whipped cream
- Sliced almonds for garnish

Instructions:

1. Place banana halves in a dish.
2. Add scoops of mocha almond fudge ice cream.
3. Drizzle with hot fudge sauce.
4. Top with whipped cream and garnish with sliced almonds.

Key Lime Pie Split

Ingredients:

- 1 banana, halved lengthwise
- 2 scoops key lime pie ice cream
- Graham cracker crumbs
- Whipped cream
- Lime zest for garnish

Instructions:

1. Place banana halves in a dish.
2. Add scoops of key lime pie ice cream.
3. Sprinkle graham cracker crumbs on top.
4. Finish with whipped cream and a sprinkle of lime zest.

Caramel Apple Split

Ingredients:

- 1 banana, halved lengthwise
- 2 scoops vanilla ice cream
- Sliced apples
- Caramel sauce
- Whipped cream
- Chopped walnuts (optional)

Instructions:

1. Place banana halves in a dish.
2. Add scoops of vanilla ice cream.
3. Top with sliced apples and drizzle with caramel sauce.
4. Finish with whipped cream and chopped walnuts if desired.

Enjoy these delicious and creative splits!

Lemon Meringue Sundae Split

Ingredients:

- 1 banana, halved lengthwise
- 2 scoops lemon sorbet
- Whipped cream
- Crushed graham crackers
- Mini meringues for topping
- Lemon zest for garnish

Instructions:

1. Place banana halves in a dish, cut side up.
2. Add scoops of lemon sorbet on top.
3. Top with whipped cream and sprinkle with crushed graham crackers.
4. Garnish with mini meringues and lemon zest.

Cookies and Cream Split

Ingredients:

- 1 banana, halved lengthwise
- 2 scoops cookies and cream ice cream
- Chocolate syrup
- Whipped cream
- Crushed chocolate cookies for garnish

Instructions:

1. Place banana halves in a dish.
2. Add scoops of cookies and cream ice cream.
3. Drizzle with chocolate syrup.
4. Top with whipped cream and sprinkle crushed chocolate cookies.

Chocolate Mint Split

Ingredients:

- 1 banana, halved lengthwise
- 2 scoops mint chocolate chip ice cream
- Hot fudge sauce
- Whipped cream
- Chocolate shavings for garnish

Instructions:

1. Place banana halves in a dish.
2. Add scoops of mint chocolate chip ice cream.
3. Drizzle with hot fudge sauce.
4. Top with whipped cream and garnish with chocolate shavings.

Maple Pecan Split

Ingredients:

- 1 banana, halved lengthwise
- 2 scoops butter pecan ice cream
- Maple syrup
- Whipped cream
- Chopped pecans for garnish

Instructions:

1. Place banana halves in a dish.
2. Add scoops of butter pecan ice cream.
3. Drizzle with maple syrup.
4. Top with whipped cream and sprinkle chopped pecans.

Cherry Cheesecake Split

Ingredients:

- 1 banana, halved lengthwise
- 2 scoops cheesecake ice cream
- Cherry topping (jarred or fresh)
- Whipped cream
- Crushed graham crackers for garnish

Instructions:

1. Place banana halves in a dish.
2. Add scoops of cheesecake ice cream.
3. Top with cherry topping and whipped cream.
4. Sprinkle with crushed graham crackers.

Coffee Crunch Split

Ingredients:

- 1 banana, halved lengthwise
- 2 scoops coffee ice cream
- Chocolate syrup
- Whipped cream
- Crushed coffee toffee candy for garnish

Instructions:

1. Place banana halves in a dish.
2. Add scoops of coffee ice cream.
3. Drizzle with chocolate syrup.
4. Top with whipped cream and sprinkle crushed coffee toffee candy.

Pumpkin Spice Split

Ingredients:

- 1 banana, halved lengthwise
- 2 scoops pumpkin ice cream
- Whipped cream
- Cinnamon for garnish
- Crushed gingersnap cookies for topping

Instructions:

1. Place banana halves in a dish.
2. Add scoops of pumpkin ice cream.
3. Top with whipped cream and sprinkle with cinnamon.
4. Garnish with crushed gingersnap cookies.

Tiramisu Sundae Split

Ingredients:

- 1 banana, halved lengthwise
- 2 scoops coffee ice cream
- Chocolate syrup
- Whipped cream
- Cocoa powder for garnish
- Ladyfinger cookies (optional)

Instructions:

1. Place banana halves in a dish.
2. Add scoops of coffee ice cream.
3. Drizzle with chocolate syrup.
4. Top with whipped cream, sprinkle with cocoa powder, and add ladyfinger cookies if desired.

Enjoy these delightful sundae splits!

Matcha Green Tea Split

Ingredients:

- 1 banana, halved lengthwise
- 2 scoops matcha green tea ice cream
- Sweetened condensed milk (optional)
- Whipped cream
- Toasted sesame seeds for garnish

Instructions:

1. Place banana halves in a dish, cut side up.
2. Add scoops of matcha green tea ice cream on top.
3. Drizzle with sweetened condensed milk if desired.
4. Top with whipped cream and sprinkle with toasted sesame seeds.

Raspberry Sorbet Split

Ingredients:

- 1 banana, halved lengthwise
- 2 scoops raspberry sorbet
- Fresh raspberries for topping
- Whipped cream
- Mint leaves for garnish

Instructions:

1. Place banana halves in a dish.
2. Add scoops of raspberry sorbet.
3. Top with fresh raspberries and whipped cream.
4. Garnish with mint leaves.

Almond Joy Split

Ingredients:

- 1 banana, halved lengthwise
- 2 scoops coconut ice cream
- Chocolate syrup
- Chopped almonds
- Whipped cream
- Toasted coconut flakes for garnish

Instructions:

1. Place banana halves in a dish.
2. Add scoops of coconut ice cream on top.
3. Drizzle with chocolate syrup and sprinkle with chopped almonds.
4. Top with whipped cream and toasted coconut flakes.

Peanut Butter Banana Split

Ingredients:

- 1 banana, halved lengthwise
- 2 scoops vanilla ice cream
- Peanut butter, warmed
- Chocolate syrup
- Whipped cream
- Chopped peanuts for garnish

Instructions:

1. Place banana halves in a dish.
2. Add scoops of vanilla ice cream.
3. Drizzle with warmed peanut butter and chocolate syrup.
4. Top with whipped cream and sprinkle with chopped peanuts.

Pina Colada Split

Ingredients:

- 1 banana, halved lengthwise
- 2 scoops coconut ice cream
- Pineapple chunks
- Whipped cream
- Toasted coconut for garnish

Instructions:

1. Place banana halves in a dish.
2. Add scoops of coconut ice cream.
3. Top with pineapple chunks and whipped cream.
4. Garnish with toasted coconut.

Chocolate Chip Cookie Split

Ingredients:

- 1 banana, halved lengthwise
- 2 scoops vanilla ice cream
- Crumbled chocolate chip cookies
- Hot fudge sauce
- Whipped cream

Instructions:

1. Place banana halves in a dish.
2. Add scoops of vanilla ice cream.
3. Sprinkle crumbled chocolate chip cookies on top.
4. Drizzle with hot fudge sauce and top with whipped cream.

Cinnamon Roll Sundae Split

Ingredients:

- 1 banana, halved lengthwise
- 2 scoops cinnamon ice cream (or vanilla)
- Warm cinnamon roll pieces
- Cream cheese frosting (optional)
- Whipped cream
- Cinnamon for garnish

Instructions:

1. Place banana halves in a dish.
2. Add scoops of cinnamon ice cream on top.
3. Top with warm cinnamon roll pieces and drizzle with cream cheese frosting if desired.
4. Finish with whipped cream and a sprinkle of cinnamon.

Chocolate Strawberry Split

Ingredients:

- 1 banana, halved lengthwise
- 2 scoops chocolate ice cream
- Fresh strawberries, sliced
- Chocolate syrup
- Whipped cream

Instructions:

1. Place banana halves in a dish.
2. Add scoops of chocolate ice cream.
3. Top with sliced strawberries and drizzle with chocolate syrup.
4. Finish with whipped cream.

Enjoy these delicious and creative splits!

Maple Bacon Split

Ingredients:

- 1 banana, halved lengthwise
- 2 scoops vanilla ice cream
- Maple syrup
- Crispy bacon pieces
- Whipped cream
- Chopped pecans for garnish

Instructions:

1. Place banana halves in a dish, cut side up.
2. Add scoops of vanilla ice cream on top.
3. Drizzle with maple syrup and sprinkle crispy bacon pieces.
4. Top with whipped cream and chopped pecans.

Key Lime Coconut Split

Ingredients:

- 1 banana, halved lengthwise
- 2 scoops key lime pie ice cream
- Shredded coconut
- Whipped cream
- Lime zest for garnish

Instructions:

1. Place banana halves in a dish.
2. Add scoops of key lime pie ice cream.
3. Top with shredded coconut and whipped cream.
4. Garnish with lime zest.

Raspberry White Chocolate Split

Ingredients:

- 1 banana, halved lengthwise
- 2 scoops white chocolate raspberry ice cream
- Fresh raspberries
- Raspberry sauce
- Whipped cream
- White chocolate shavings for garnish

Instructions:

1. Place banana halves in a dish.
2. Add scoops of white chocolate raspberry ice cream.
3. Top with fresh raspberries and drizzle with raspberry sauce.
4. Finish with whipped cream and white chocolate shavings.

Dark Chocolate Cherry Split

Ingredients:

- 1 banana, halved lengthwise
- 2 scoops dark chocolate ice cream
- Cherry topping (jarred or fresh)
- Whipped cream
- Dark chocolate chips for garnish

Instructions:

1. Place banana halves in a dish.
2. Add scoops of dark chocolate ice cream.
3. Top with cherry topping and whipped cream.
4. Sprinkle with dark chocolate chips.

Pistachio Dream Split

Ingredients:

- 1 banana, halved lengthwise
- 2 scoops pistachio ice cream
- Chopped pistachios
- Whipped cream
- Drizzle of honey for garnish

Instructions:

1. Place banana halves in a dish.
2. Add scoops of pistachio ice cream.
3. Top with chopped pistachios and whipped cream.
4. Drizzle with honey.

Orange Creamsicle Split

Ingredients:

- 1 banana, halved lengthwise
- 2 scoops orange sherbet
- Vanilla ice cream
- Whipped cream
- Orange zest for garnish

Instructions:

1. Place banana halves in a dish.
2. Add scoops of orange sherbet and vanilla ice cream on top.
3. Top with whipped cream.
4. Garnish with orange zest.

Snickers Sundae Split

Ingredients:

- 1 banana, halved lengthwise
- 2 scoops chocolate ice cream
- Chopped Snickers bars
- Caramel sauce
- Whipped cream
- Chopped peanuts for garnish

Instructions:

1. Place banana halves in a dish.
2. Add scoops of chocolate ice cream.
3. Top with chopped Snickers bars and drizzle with caramel sauce.
4. Finish with whipped cream and chopped peanuts.

Lemon Basil Split

Ingredients:

- 1 banana, halved lengthwise
- 2 scoops lemon sorbet
- Fresh basil leaves
- Whipped cream
- Lemon zest for garnish

Instructions:

1. Place banana halves in a dish.
2. Add scoops of lemon sorbet on top.
3. Top with fresh basil leaves and whipped cream.
4. Garnish with lemon zest.

Enjoy these refreshing and indulgent splits!

Red Velvet Cake Split

Ingredients:

- 1 banana, halved lengthwise
- 2 scoops cream cheese ice cream
- Crumbled red velvet cake
- Whipped cream
- Chocolate shavings for garnish

Instructions:

1. Place banana halves in a dish, cut side up.
2. Add scoops of cream cheese ice cream on top.
3. Sprinkle crumbled red velvet cake over the ice cream.
4. Top with whipped cream and garnish with chocolate shavings.

Fudge Brownie Split

Ingredients:

- 1 banana, halved lengthwise
- 2 scoops chocolate fudge ice cream
- Brownie pieces
- Hot fudge sauce
- Whipped cream
- Chopped nuts for garnish

Instructions:

1. Place banana halves in a dish.
2. Add scoops of chocolate fudge ice cream.
3. Top with brownie pieces and drizzle with hot fudge sauce.
4. Finish with whipped cream and chopped nuts.

Coconut Cream Pie Split

Ingredients:

- 1 banana, halved lengthwise
- 2 scoops coconut ice cream
- Coconut whipped cream
- Toasted coconut flakes
- Graham cracker crumbs for garnish

Instructions:

1. Place banana halves in a dish.
2. Add scoops of coconut ice cream on top.
3. Top with coconut whipped cream and toasted coconut flakes.
4. Sprinkle with graham cracker crumbs.

Orange Mango Split

Ingredients:

- 1 banana, halved lengthwise
- 2 scoops mango sorbet
- 1 scoop orange sherbet
- Whipped cream
- Fresh mango slices for garnish

Instructions:

1. Place banana halves in a dish.
2. Add scoops of mango sorbet and orange sherbet.
3. Top with whipped cream and garnish with fresh mango slices.

Vanilla Almond Joy Split

Ingredients:

- 1 banana, halved lengthwise
- 2 scoops vanilla ice cream
- Chocolate syrup
- Almonds
- Whipped cream
- Toasted coconut flakes for garnish

Instructions:

1. Place banana halves in a dish.
2. Add scoops of vanilla ice cream.
3. Drizzle with chocolate syrup and sprinkle with almonds.
4. Top with whipped cream and toasted coconut flakes.

Tropical Paradise Split

Ingredients:

- 1 banana, halved lengthwise
- 2 scoops pineapple coconut ice cream
- Fresh pineapple chunks
- Whipped cream
- Maraschino cherry for garnish

Instructions:

1. Place banana halves in a dish.
2. Add scoops of pineapple coconut ice cream.
3. Top with fresh pineapple chunks and whipped cream.
4. Finish with a maraschino cherry on top.

Enjoy these delightful and creative splits!

Butterscotch Pecan Split

Ingredients:

- 1 banana, halved lengthwise
- 2 scoops vanilla ice cream
- Butterscotch sauce
- Chopped pecans
- Whipped cream
- Caramel sauce for garnish

Instructions:

1. Place banana halves in a dish, cut side up.
2. Add scoops of vanilla ice cream on top.
3. Drizzle with butterscotch sauce and sprinkle chopped pecans.
4. Top with whipped cream and a drizzle of caramel sauce.

Strawberry Cheesecake Split

Ingredients:

- 1 banana, halved lengthwise
- 2 scoops strawberry cheesecake ice cream
- Fresh strawberries, sliced
- Whipped cream
- Graham cracker crumbs for garnish

Instructions:

1. Place banana halves in a dish.
2. Add scoops of strawberry cheesecake ice cream.
3. Top with sliced strawberries and whipped cream.
4. Sprinkle with graham cracker crumbs.

Chocolate Coconut Split

Ingredients:

- 1 banana, halved lengthwise
- 2 scoops chocolate coconut ice cream
- Hot fudge sauce
- Whipped cream
- Toasted coconut flakes for garnish

Instructions:

1. Place banana halves in a dish.
2. Add scoops of chocolate coconut ice cream.
3. Drizzle with hot fudge sauce.
4. Top with whipped cream and toasted coconut flakes.

Vanilla Bourbon Split

Ingredients:

- 1 banana, halved lengthwise
- 2 scoops vanilla ice cream
- Bourbon caramel sauce (made with bourbon, sugar, and cream)
- Whipped cream
- Crushed pecans for garnish

Instructions:

1. Place banana halves in a dish.
2. Add scoops of vanilla ice cream on top.
3. Drizzle with bourbon caramel sauce.
4. Top with whipped cream and crushed pecans.

Enjoy these indulgent and delicious splits!